MARRIED/SINGULAR

Also by Philip Oakes

POEMS
In the Affirmative
Unlucky Jonah

NOVELS
Experiment at Proto
The God Botherers
Exactly What We Want

MARRIED/SINGULAR

Philip Oakes

ANDRE DEUTSCH

First published 1973 by
André Deutsch Limited
105 Great Russell Street, London WC1

Copyright © 1973 by Philip Oakes

Printed in Great Britain by
Clarke, Doble and Brendon Ltd
Plymouth

ISBN 0 233 96450 9

Some of these poems previously appeared
in *The London Magazine*, *The Sunday
Times*, *The New Statesman*, *The Listener*
and *Transatlantic Review*. 'Girl on a Bus'
was commissioned and is performed by The
Barrow Poets.

CONTENTS

1

Daniel Lambert	9
Mr Valobra	11
Bones	12
Live Baiting	13
The Old Words	14
Notes by the Provincial Governor	15
Company	17
From the Train	19
Girl on a Bus	20
Inside	21
A New Leaf	23
Miss America! Miss America!	25
The Black Dog	26

2

The Tea Ceremony	31
Bed Making	32
Firelighting	33
A Hot Iron	34
Gardening Poem	35
Whodunit	36
Do It Yourself	37
Taking a Bath	38
The Midnight Movie	39
Spiders	40
In the Kitchen	41
Guarantee	43

1

DANIEL LAMBERT

Daniel Lambert, a corpulent gentleman
Weighing upwards of fifty stone,
But nonetheless genial, athletic, and polite
Was walking with his dog in Leicester
When he met a dancing bear.
The dog bit Bruin. Bruin's master
Beat the dog, and Mr Lambert
Hastened to the rescue of his pet.
In vain : the bear threw Mr Lambert down,
And there he lay, unable to regain his feet.
    Some people laughed (a fat man on his back
Is comical). But Mr Lambert bore it well.
He knew himself to be a *personage*,
Of normal size until the age of twenty,
After which he grew and grew
Into a figure, not of fun, but dignity.
His health was excellent, his strength
Proportionate to his appearance.
He shouldered hundredweights, bred hounds,
And fighting cocks, swam sturdily
In sea and lake, conversed with wit,
And won the hearts and high esteem
Of all who spoke with him.
Callers were welcome at his London home :
Price of admission, one shilling.
    He called himself the heaviest man
In England, supping on water
While his bulk increased.
One evening in the year 1809
Nature rebelled against the trespass
She had borne so long. The clogged machinery
Of life stood still, this prodigy of mammon
Breathed his last, and on his couch

Lay numbered with the dead.
　　　His coffin, made of elm, stood on two axle-trees
And four clog-wheels. The church
Could not accomodate its width,
And eight men lugged it to the burial-ground.
The rest was briskly done :
The grave-yard gulped it down,
The sexton tucked the turf in place,
And worms began their surgery.
　　　Now he is liberated from the flesh,
His buoyant spirit races free.
Send your prayers coursing after Daniel Lambert's soul.
In heaven he's no weight at all.

MR VALOBRA

Poor Mr Valobra, he sees gaps
In the pavement where there are no gaps.
He walks the streets remarkably slow
And peaceable, winter and summer,
Wearing greatcoat and boots,
A stick in his hand. He smiles
And talks to himself, but then
He stops short. He is in fear
Of falling into a pit. A friend
Accosts him: 'How are you Mr Valobra?'
'Very well Sir, if it were not for these
                                    cursed gaps.'
When young he was handsome.
Indeed, his present figure amply denotes
Superior deportment and a noble cast
Of feature. For years he was an inmate
Of a private madhouse, padded and barred.
The hardships he endured still lock his tongue.
Relations urge him to stay at home. A carriage
Is available, attendants have been offered.
But Mr Valobra says no. He travels safely
In the midst of danger. He feels happy
In no other recreation.
'Are your father and friends well, Sir?'
'Yes, all's well. But – never mind,
For it's right and wrong all over the world.'

BONES

We keep digging up bones, broken tiles,
Clay pipes embossed with anchors,
Bottles of liniment, pram wheels.

Today my fork went through a pig-skull,
Piercing the cranium and lifting it,
Tobacco-brown and whole.

There was no corruption, no dead meat.
Corn glared through the empty sockets,
Earth had sucked it sweet.

I set it eighteen inches down
To await decay or the next spade
To turn when we are gone.

I felt no grub in the mind
Twitching towards immortality. Only
The question : will we leave as much behind?

LIVE BAITING

It isn't nice, the way I fish:
Kidnapping roach from quiet ponds,
And spitting them on hooks
For pike to eat.
They swim, you could say, freely; live bait,
Unconstrained by locks,
But tethered by lip or fin, their bonds
Almost invisible, the barbs buried in flesh.

Each cast gives them the chance
To die. Scalded by air
They plummet thirty yards upstream,
Bombing the shallows, targets
That swim into the sights
Of what will kill them.
Pike aren't interested in playing at war,
They meet their partners in an older dance.

The one I caught today wore
Like a brooch a hook of mine, lost
When the line broke months ago.
I found it rooted
In her throat. When I gutted
Her, eggs lined her belly like orange sago.
Pain has no memory, grief stays in the past.
It isn't true. I can't fish this way any more.

THE OLD WORDS

There are expressions gentler
Than 'getting it up' and 'ramming it home',
But few, perhaps, more vivid.
Saying the words you actually see
The nodding phallus ripe with blood
Commit its merry rape;
The phrases stir both lust and poetry.

Blue movies have nothing
On the printed page and print itself
Leaves out the best part:
The precise pitch at which she screams
'I'm coming' – what you might call
The personal note, a song
To warm your desert island dreams.

It isn't literature
And much too limiting to suit
The fly pornographer – no creamy thighs,
No lesbian couplings, or whips.
These words which nip the inner ear
Come from a plainer time,
Were spelled by older lips.

In caves maybe, in bivouacs,
On beds of rushes, firelight capping
The fool and drowsy hawk.
They are secreted by the bone's marrow,
Remembered like spells and said
To salt our daily bread. Repeat them now
And taste yourself a hero.

NOTES BY THE PROVINCIAL
GOVERNOR

This day in June my pond contains
Two golden orfe, four tench,
Two stickleback, eleven roach,
Inumerable small-fry (swollen-headed, sharp as tacks),
Beetles and daphnia, snails,
And algae thick as syllabub,
A broth to nourish great and small.

I have planted lilies, a water soldier,
Weed to distil oxygen,
Set rocks and pebbles, spinneys
Of green to clad the landscape.
What more do they need?
I have promised to rule justly;
Might has its obligations.

August. Returning from leave
I note the level of the pond has fallen.
Fortify banks, increase security.
Swallows patrol the surface, sieving
The air. I praise their vigilance.
Last night a rat broke the perimeter;
Soon he will feed on poison.

I do not understand my subjects:
In winter I melt holes in the ice,
I chop worms for their food.
They are not grateful. The shoals reject
My hand, my shadow makes them flinch.
They prosper but they will not bring
Their children to be blessed.

October. God lives! His plague
Has fallen on the pond. A growth
Like muslin chokes the waterways.
There is no *lebensraum*. Life is a maze
Of soft, blind alleys. Their fault, theirs.
I grant them self-determination.
Now I shall found another colony.

COMPANY

Looking cross-country I suddenly saw
The hills I had thought
Resembled a lion's paws
Were the actual paws of a beast,
So large that his head and torso
Were lost in cloud,
And the scribbles of briar
Were strands of mane
Endorsing his endless pelt.

I was not deceived. The world
Was suddenly made plain.
Legends were true, the landscape reformed.
When the wind blew
I saw the green man walk, verdant
And mailed in beech-leaf and alder.
The gossip of owls became clear:
Death was their topic, their bone to pick
With keener relish than the mice
They swallowed whole.

The river washed the weedy hair
Of suicides. The hill unrolled
Like a night safe, coughing up
Its hoard of Saxon gold.
The sky was thronged with men
And animals, burning like stars,
Burning and then extinguishing themselves,
Slowly as cinders, or spitting out
Their lives like cigarettes in water.

I was surrounded by ghosts and guardians,
The air was populous, the fields inhabited.

We share quarters with more than we know:
Family, friends, familiars.
And how many more attend us?
How many more watch over us?

FROM THE TRAIN

You will never find the place on foot;
Fields defend it, the trees
Have been trained to move in clumps,
That spinney acting as decoy
While the other flits out of view.

The house also can disappear at will;
Timbers and brick dissolving,
The roof soaking
Into the sky, leaving no stain
For birds to bump into.

Trust in the fact that when you've gone
Everything will reassemble; chimneys
Reconstitute themselves, roots
Carry on drinking, clouds cross the horizon,
All of summer will continue.

What you have seen is a memory
Glimpsed from a train as England unspools
Between orchards and quarries like cut-cake,
And meres ornamented with swans
Slide past the window.

Even if you alight at the next station,
Consult maps and offer bribes,
No one can help you.
Back, further back, they'll say,
Pointing past signal box and junction.

The place you seek is behind you.

GIRL ON A BUS

Straphanging this summer afternoon
I lurched when the bus lurched
And found myself tilted like beer
In a bottle, gravely studying
The furrow in your hair,
The downward slope of your nose,
The pleat in your sunburned chest.

It was like opening a door marked Private,
Or glancing through a porthole
The moment a dolphin jumps.

The view came and went.
The bus righted itself;
Perspective was restored.

Sitting at home I nurse my equilibrium,
But, steady as I go, the prospect returns.
I see the door open, the dolphin
Endlessly diving. So, for the record
I write it down. Today's vision:
An accident, a promise, an infinity of flesh,
Brought to you, and you, and you,
By courtesy of London Transport.

INSIDE

Africa's inside you, wild things
And flowers which grow like meat.
The air's a poultice,
Even the sun is wet.
On this gold coast orchids have tongues,
The mangrove wades in blood
And grasses make their vegetable din.
They utter love. Torn branches bud,
Paths open up, then tightly close again.
The country heals itself,
Yielding to maps, remaining virgin.

Inside and out you are a landscape.
Your flanks are limestone, your body fleece
Is pasture, grass to fatten sheep.
You harbour all that's various
In weather and geography.
You are a sample pack of continents.
Tropics, savannahs, salt water and fresh. I lie
Here, breathing your body scents,
Meddling with lava, making new.
In time all things resemble you.

Uplands, lowlands, that sweet hole in the ground
Smoking with bees,
Hauling their freight from dawn to dusk,
Pollen packed behind their knees,
Their wings drilling dimples of sound
In the afternoon.
Their hoard is honey, bottled in wax.
Your juices run
More easily, summer and winter, a flux

Of nature, butting through time and stone,
A spring which never locks.

Drinking deeply, pacing the sand,
I feel like Crusoe, here for a spell,
Bound to be taken off by the unplanned
Boat making its landfall.
Others will come with measures and plumb-lines,
Drilling the soil, planting seed,
Sending love to the generations.
I send mine also. They won't need
Directions. Each settler must find his own.
Offer no help, cover all tracks. Tell them love is exploration.

A NEW LEAF

I look forward to next year's diary
In which your name will not appear.
The lamp you gave me is broken,
The sheets have been laundered
And yesterday I woke, made tea
And shaved before remembering
That you were dead.
        The healing process has begun
And what mends first is flesh.
Some veterans of World War One
Go round with shrapnel
Lodged in them like pips. The body
Puts itself together. Tissue knits,
But nothing is the same.
        I feel grief like a stitch
In the side, sense it like a missing stair.
You are safe in the context of time;
There's a before and after.
But, in between, I see you still:
Your heavy breasts, your waist toboganning
Into a bank of bone, your cockled toes,
Your hair spilling like water.
        You are printed on me
Like a leaf in stone, a transfer
Of what's gone. Your absence
Has an outline and I conform to it.
With my eyes open or shut
I read you like braille.
        I can forget dates, anniversaries,
Your recollected face already looks
Less like your photograph.
But in the dark-room of my mind the series
Endlessly extends, editions multiply.

No diary can keep you out.
You fill each empty page, cancelling time,
Making your mark again, again, again,
Raging with love against the day
That dares to post you missing.

MISS AMERICA! MISS AMERICA!

Cases of Pepsi, vats of Seven-Up, white bread chewy as gum,
Marshmallows, hot pallid franks, ketchup, and Hershey bars,

Dino and Dylan, J. D. Salinger, in whom
A generation put its trust, only to lose

It when JC or his agent took the lease,
Meekly enduring cancer and piles, not a Jewish saint but
    Asian,

Soggy with love like the Maharishi, and gutless.
I think of your component parts, the mind mulching
    information,

Turning it into sileage; the stomach processing hard tack
And soft; the wrapping by Brooks Brothers, Bloomingdale,
    or Levi.

Making love to you is by courtesy of whichever eunuch
Presses the button. It is like screwing the consumer society.

THE BLACK DOG

By taking this tablet I can exchange
One bad dream for another:
No sleep for sleep bruised by nightmares;
The maundering of clocks for a movie
Inside my skull, non-linear,
Bleeding from jump cuts, wholly irrational.
There's always a choice, but choosing either/or
I elect for punishment, not relief.

Gulping one down is easy, the risk
Is what you make it. Goering played host
To cyanide bonded in plastic, tough as a louse's egg,
Safe to swallow, void and cycle back
Until the day he sensed the hangman
Gauging his weight and doing deadly sums.
The Marshal sought his medicine,
Bit hard and took it neat.

I've thought about it often, but the shit
That Goering wiped away has entered
The prescription. There are no aids
To gracious dying, nothing to manufacture
Sleep that's worry-free. The black dog begs
His meat and rather than see him starve
We offer scraps, a warm corner, equal shares.
Devotedly he pays us back, the going rate.

Tonight I feel his breath basting my neck,
His tongue scooping out my ear like a cornet.
He is no one's pet, cannot be kept in quarantine,
We suffer his distemper like our own.

The tablets cure nothing but still we take them,
Measure for measure, tit for tat.
The black dog guards our dreams;
We plan survival on a balanced diet.

2

THE TEA CEREMONY

First warm the pot, making sure
That the water is boiling. Measure the tea,
And take the pot to the kettle, never the
Kettle to the pot; observe procedure.
Each household has its god or demon
To placate, and today
Is a good time to start. Do it this way.
Offer a choice of milk or lemon,
Either will do. The Japanese
Make a ritual of drinking tea,
Scalding each leaf singly,
Watching their lives unfold. Our way is
Less finicky, but just as meaningful.
Pledging fragments, we redeem the whole.

BED MAKING

This mattress has a thousand springs,
Each one supports an ounce or so,
Bracing shoulder, hip and toe,
Keeping the spine level, heart and lungs
Ticking over as they should.

We chose it together. Three children,
Two living, one dead
Were conceived here. On this bed
Have lain cats, dogs with muddy paws. Our son
Was born squalling on the far side.

Meanwhile, in another room, his sister sung
An evening hymn. The nurse
Had lost her scissors.
Waiting for no one he barged his way out, a strong
Boy, meaty as an Oxo cube.

We love our ghosts. How many haunt
This cockpit, bloody and seeded?
Now we make hospital corners as we made
Love, out of habit, out of want.
This is our bed, and we must lie on it.

FIRELIGHTING

It's my job to make the fire,
Laying the foundations with paper and sticks,
Balancing small coals on the scaffold,
Setting it alight with just one match.
More chancy than the kitchen boiler,
Sucking at anthracite and bricks
Of coal dust, changing sullen black to gold.
Open fires are livelier to watch.

The pictures they form continually change:
Sheer cliffs of flame are drilled
By salamanders, pot-holes appear,
Faces materialize, and then decay.
Perhaps our lives are there, a range
Of happenings to build
Into a blaze, an opportunity to play with fire
And not get burned. Perhaps it is the only way.

A HOT IRON

Sailing on a sea of poplin
This craft crushes ripples flat.
It steams on, leaving behind it
A calm sea, everything serene.

There are no doldrums here,
The sky is washday bright.
Cracking in the wind, white
Sheets welcome fair weather.

A safe passage. Your holy iron,
Your rough waters shrive
All dirty linen. They remove
Stains, giving absolution.

For seven days at least;
Goodness endures that long.
Scorch marks, and a smell of burning
Persist, telling us that we are blessed.

GARDENING POEM

8 a. m. and the beans are ready for inspection;
No blackfly, no dingy leaves, all's well.
The sun moves on, the shadows wheel,
The garden, like a clock-face, tells the time.
Strawberries stand at ten,
Sweet-corn at eleven, roses punctuate the day.
You dig potatoes, weed the radishes,
Cut mint, bind honeysuckle.
This is your platoon, your ward, your parish;
In an election they would vote for you.
Always, by God, you tend your troops
Before seeking your own quarters,
Watering them, bedding them down.
They'll honour you; love pollinates
All that it touches. Your hands are diligent.
Your fingers pinch, pluck, curry, and groom.
This year the yield will be heavy. Harvest,
You say, begins at home.

WHODUNIT

Who/what killed the marrow?
Three weeks growing, green shoulders spreading
Into palms which said *Oi Veh* !
A vegetable Shylock, dying in circumstances
Far from kosher.
        Line up the suspects : rain
Dripping from the roof, bead after bead,
Like Chinese water torture; slugs
(The little silver ones, plated in slime);
East winds, chopping the blossom;
Cats, digging their small latrines.
        Each, and any one of these
Could be guilty. Your vigilance will seek
Him out. You have a nose for malefactors.
When you ask questions
Evil curls up like a wood-louse.
        What you seek to attach is blame,
Hanging it round the culprit's neck
Like a clapper, a bell which cries unclean.
There is no other penalty.
It's enough for you – and so the world – to know
Whodunit (the cat as it happens).
Why is not important to your case.
        This marrow died in a good cause.
Virtue was seen to win again. The garden
Will sleep more easily tonight.

DO IT YOURSELF

Don't ask me to mend things.
Once, my woodwork teacher marked
Me three out of three hundred, proof,
He said, of his Christian charity.
Everyone laughed, toadies all;
The class knew I was not practical.

Nor am I now. Washers and springs
Defeat me. So do tumblers gripping locked
Doors. I don't know enough
About currents to fool with electricity.
There's a gap between my brain and hand
Transcending clumsiness. I do not understand.

This blind bulb, those tipsy palings,
That chest of drawers pocked
By a blunt chisel call my bluff.
Each one is entered as a casualty.
I damage more than I can ever mend;
Make your repairs, heal the wound.

TAKING A BATH

To rest in warm water, the pumice
Bobbing between my legs, watching
The course of tame tides
Sluicing through hair and canting the loofah
Is a kind of happiness
Like convalescence, a reward for catching
Cold, kinder than medicine or bromides,
Solace for pain, without having had to suffer.

Water bears the weight. My penis
Lolls in the surf, winking its eye
Above the spot where I lie sunk.
Gladly I come apart. My fingers flex,
Soft as anemones
Groping for food. I am at sea
On dry land. Fish nibble at my trunk,
And tug me down among the other wrecks.

Embryos live like this, moored
To their mothers, nuggets of gristle and yolk.
Their gills dissolve, their fingers sprout like buds.
And yet, from fish to human flesh,
The form's not final. Cured
Of the first condition, we invoke
Another, still imperfect. Marinating in these suds,
I pray that everything will come out in the wash.

THE MIDNIGHT MOVIE

Garland dances, Peck and Heston fight
To a draw in a moon-washed meadow.
Late night movies pit
Our substance against their shadow.

The heroes have not changed. Bogart still wears
His trench coat, Dooley Wilson plays
As Time Goes By. Their spent years
Go more slowly than our days.

Between us and them
There's no closing up; the distance is
The same before and after the programme.
We never meet face to face.

It's just as well. Those lovers kissing now
Lie deep in Forest Lawn, their profiles
Mangier than twenty years ago
When we admired them from the stalls.

The television set is haunted:
Not by the tenants, but the hosts.
We turn the reels of what we wanted,
Watched by our own ghosts.

SPIDERS

Why does she like spiders?
Bitty as beads, fat as comfits,
Treading the air in kitchen and bathroom,
Shinning up pipes to strand themselves
In porcelain wastelands:
What's the attraction?

She argues: they have personality.
I wouldn't know,
I've never talked to one.
Each autumn they invade my house,
Cramming their eggs in corners,
Cosy as cotton-wool inside an ear.

They pay their way. Each window
Is a boneyard. What I resent
(Not on behalf of flies)
Is their stupidity. They drown
In puddles, roast in burning logs:
It's carelessness, not suicide.

And yet she grieves.
These juicy yo-yos, mithering their young
Are all her creatures.
Cats may not kill them,
Birds are given crumbs.
Careful, she says, here comes a big one.

IN THE KITCHEN

You make chapels of bread,
Temples of pastry, incense
Breathes from your oven.
You anoint birds with bacon,
Puddings with brandy, dead
Meat stirs and quickens
In your casserole, herbs leaven
Flesh, prising it from the bone.

You deal in resurrection;
Elements renew themselves.
Sugar reverts to sap, eggs bloom
Into soufflés, parsley veins
Fish like marble. Nothing and no one
Leaves your hand unchanged. Kidneys, calves'
Liver, bits from the body's boiler-room
Are made over. You restore innocence.

My mother's soup had beads
Of fat like seed pearls, strung
On the surface, jewelling the spoon.
'Not grease' she always said,
'But goodness', rendering down all creeds
To one affirmative, a tincture strong
As garlic, evident as saffron:
What we eat, we are. On this we fed.

We feed there still. Receipts
Are honoured in this house.
Not written down, but hopefully believed.
They are the only charms allowed:

We trust in them. Our debts
Discourage speculation. Prayers
Are not the rafts on which we shall be saved.
We say no grace. We seek it in our food.

GUARANTEE

You are veined like a leaf.
Babies have tenderized your breasts,
Munching the tissue with their bony gums.
        Your fingers are scored
By chopping knives, the oven door,
Hot fat, and rose thorns.
        No one would call
You beautiful. Your hair is brindled
By time and weather,
        Your skin is foxed
Like a first edition. You show
Distinct signs of wear and tear.
        Cats sleep in your lap,
Children come to have their noses blown.
You keep secrets like a strong box.
        You are not for special
Occasions, but for everyday. You have
The virtues of denim, wholemeal, and worsted.
        You are durable.
You bring words out of storage,
And on your lips they do not sound strange.
        Love, duty, service:
Sturdier than slipwear, but with the same
Patina, the same hair-line cracks.
        In your house, though,
They are for use, and not display.
They are not allowed to gather dust.
        You are not one
For ornaments. They break easily
Or get in the way.
        You prefer shelves, tables,
Lives to be uncluttered. Without distraction
Wood shows its grain, glass its sparkle.

You are happiest
When nothing goes remarked, and celebration
Is the act itself.
        You are patient with people,
And implements, you can tie knots,
And start engines. Vegetables grow for you.
        I will not praise you, beyond saying
That you are able, amiable, and welcome.
You meet all guarantees. You are as promised.